STREET SONGS

STREET SONGS

BY
EDITH SITWELL

LONDON
MACMILLAN & CO. LTD
1943

COPYRIGHT

First Edition, January 1942
Reprinted February and May 1942
April 1943

PRINTED IN GREAT BRITAIN
BY R. & R. CLARK, LIMITED, EDINBURGH

TO
OSBERT SITWELL

ACKNOWLEDGMENTS

My thanks are due to Messrs. Faber & Faber for their kind permission to include " Lullaby " and " Serenade," from *Poems Old and New* ; to the Editor of *The Times Literary Supplement* for kindly allowing me to reproduce " Lullaby " and " Still Falls the Rain " ; and to the Editor of *Life and Letters To-Day* for his kindness in allowing " Street Song," " Tattered Serenade," " The Youth with the Red-Gold Hair," " Song " (" We are the darkness in the heat of the day "), " Poor Young Simpleton," " An Old Song Re-sung," and " Once my heart was a summer rose " to be included.

E. S.

CONTENTS

	PAGE
STILL FALLS THE RAIN	1
LULLABY	3
SERENADE: ANY MAN TO ANY WOMAN . .	5
STREET SONG	7
POOR YOUNG SIMPLETON:	
I. (An Old Song Re-sung)	9
II. (". . . damné par l'arc-en-ciel") . .	10
SONG: Once my heart was a summer rose . .	13
TATTERED SERENADE: BEGGAR TO SHADOW:	
I. These are the nations of the Dead, their million-year-old	15
II. In the summer, when noone is cold . .	18
TEARS	20
THE FLOWERING FOREST	21
HOW MANY HEAVENS	22
SPRING	23
YOU, THE YOUNG RAINBOW	24
SONG: We are the darkness in the heat of the day .	25
THE YOUTH WITH THE RED-GOLD HAIR . .	26
THE NIGHT BEFORE GREAT BABYLON . . .	27
SONG: When I was but a child, that Lion . .	28
MOST LOVELY SHADE	29
THE WEEPING ROSE	30
THE SWANS	31
AN OLD WOMAN	32

Still Falls the Rain

(THE RAIDS, 1940. NIGHT AND DAWN)

STILL falls the Rain—
Dark as the world of man, black as our loss—
Blind as the nineteen hundred and forty nails
Upon the Cross.

Still falls the Rain
With a sound like the pulse of the heart that is changed
                                      to the hammer-beat
In the Potter's Field, and the sound of the impious feet

On the Tomb :
          Still falls the Rain
In the Field of Blood where the small hopes breed and
                                the human brain
Nurtures its greed, that worm with the brow of Cain.

Still falls the Rain
At the feet of the Starved Man hung upon the Cross.
Christ that each day, each night, nails there,
                          have mercy on us—
On Dives and on Lazarus :
Under the Rain the sore and the gold are as one.

Still falls the Rain—
Still falls the Blood from the Starved Man's wounded Side :
He bears in His Heart all wounds,—those of the light
                          that died,
The last faint spark
In the self-murdered heart, the wounds of the sad
                                uncomprehending dark,

The wounds of the baited bear,—
The blind and weeping bear whom the keepers beat
On his helpless flesh . . . the tears of the hunted hare.

Still falls the Rain—
Then—O Ile leape up to my God: who pulles me doune—
See, see where Christ's blood streames in the firmament:
It flows from the Brow we nailed upon the tree
Deep to the dying, to the thirsting heart
That holds the fires of the world,—dark-smirched with pain
As Caesar's laurel crown.

Then sounds the voice of One who like the heart of man
Was once a child who among beasts has lain—
" Still do I love, still shed my innocent light, my Blood,
                                                              for thee."

Lullaby

Though the world has slipped and gone,
Sounds my loud discordant cry
Like the steel birds' song on high:
"Still one thing is left—the Bone!"
Then out danced the Babioun.

She sat in the hollow of the sea—
A socket whence the eye's put out—
She sang to the child a lullaby
(The steel birds' nest was thereabout).

"Do, do, do, do—
Thy mother's hied to the vaster race:
The Pterodactyl made its nest
And laid a steel egg in her breast—
Under the Judas-coloured sun.
She'll work no more, nor dance, nor moan,
And I am come to take her place
Do, do.

There's nothing left but earth's low bed—
(The Pterodactyl fouls its nest):
But steel wings fan thee to thy rest,
And wingless truth and larvae lie
And eyeless hope and handless fear—
All these for thee as toys are spread,
Do—do—

Note.—The phrase "out-dance the Babioun" occurs in an Epigram by Ben Jonson.

Red is the bed of Poland, Spain,
And thy mother's breast, who has grown wise
In that fouled nest. If she could rise,
Give birth again,

In wolfish pelt she'd hide thy bones
To shield thee from the world's long cold,
And down on all fours shouldst thou crawl
For thus from no height canst thou fall —
Do, do.

She'd give no hands : there's nought to hold
And nought to make : there's dust to sift,
But no food for the hands to lift.
Do, do.

Heed my ragged lullaby,
Fear not living, fear not chance ;
All is equal — blindness, sight,
There is no depth, there is no height :
Do, do,

The Judas-coloured sun is gone,
And with the Ape thou art alone —
Do,
    Do."

Serenade: Any Man to Any Woman

DARK angel who art clear and straight
As cannon shining in the air,
Your blackness doth invade my mind
And thunderous as the armoured wind
That rained on Europe is your hair;

And so I love you till I die —
(Unfaithful I, the cannon's mate):
Forgive my love of such brief span,
But fickle is the flesh of man,
And death's cold puts the passion out.

I'll woo you with a serenade —
The wolfish howls the starving made;
And lies shall be your canopy
To shield you from the freezing sky.

Yet when I clasp you in my arms —
Who are my sleep, the zero hour
That clothes, instead of flesh, my heart, —
You in my heaven have no part,
For you, my mirage broken in flower,

Can never see what dead men know!
Then die with me and be my love:
The grave shall be your shady grove
And in your pleasaunce rivers flow

(To ripen this new Paradise)
From a more universal Flood
Than Noah knew: but yours is blood.

Yet still you will imperfect be
That in my heart like death's chill grows,
—A rainbow shining in the night,
Born of my tears . . . your lips, the bright
Summer-old folly of the rose.

Street Song

" LOVE my heart for an hour, but my bone for a day—
At least the skeleton smiles, for it has a morrow :
But the hearts of the young are now the dark treasure
                                     of Death,
And summer is lonely.

Comfort the lonely light and the sun in its sorrow,
Come like the night, for terrible is the sun
As truth, and the dying light shows only the
                                     skeleton's hunger
For peace, under the flesh like the summer rose.

Come through the darkness of death, as once through
                                     the branches
Of youth you came, through the shade like the
                                     flowering door
That leads into Paradise, far from the street,—you,
                                     the unborn
City seen by the homeless, the night of the poor.

You walk in the city ways, where Man's threatening shadow
Red-edged by the sun like Cain, has a changing shape—
Elegant like the Skeleton, crouched like the Tiger,
With the age-old wisdom and aptness of the Ape.

The pulse that beats in the heart is changed to the hammer
That sounds in the Potter's Field where they build
                                     a new world
From our Bone, and the carrion-bird days' foul droppings
                                     and clamour—
But you are my night, and my peace,—

The holy night of conception, of rest, the consoling
Darkness when all men are equal,—the wrong and the right,
And the rich and the poor are no longer separate nations,—
They are brothers in night."

This was the song I heard ; but the Bone is silent !
Who knows if the sound was that of the dead light calling,—
Of Caesar rolling onward his heart, that stone,
Or the burden of Atlas falling.

Poor Young Simpleton

I

An Old Song Re-sung

" Once my love seemed the Burning Bush,
The Pentecost Rushing of Flames :
Now the Speech has fallen to the chatter of alleys
Where fallen man and the rising ape
And the howling Dark play games.

For she leaned from the light like the Queen of Fairies
Out of the bush of the yellow broom . . .
' I'll take out that heart of yours,' she said,
' And put in your breast a stone.
O, I'll leave an empty room,' she said,
' A fouled, but an empty room.' "

Poor Young Simpleton

II

"... *damné par l'arc-en-ciel*"

("Saison en Enfer")

"I WALKED with my dead living love in the city—
The Potter's Field where the race of Man
Constructs a new world with hands thumbless from unuse
—(Pads like a tiger's)—a skeleton plan.

We walked in the city where even the lightning—
The Flag of Blood flying across the world,
The Flag of immeasurable Doom, of God's warning,
Is changed to a spider's universe, furled

For a banner of hunger . . . the world of the thunder
Is dulled till it seems but the idiot drum
Of a universe changed to a circus,—the clatter
Where the paralysed dance in the blind man's slum.

But the sun was huge as a mountain of diamonds
That starved men see on a plain far away:
It will never buy food, but its red fires glittered
On the Heart of Quietness, my Eden day.

For she was the cool of the evening, bringing
The dead child home to the mother's breast,
The wanderer homeward, far from the hammer
That beats in the Potter's Field: she was my rest,

And the Burning Bush, and the worker's Sunday,
The neighbour of Silence, speech to the still,
And her kiss was the Fiery Chariot, low swinging
To take me over the diamond hill.

Where the crowds sweep onward, mountaineers, nomads
From cities and continents man has not seen,
With beachcombers drifted from shores that no wave
                                                   has known,
Pilgrims to shrines where no God-head has been,

We watched the sonambulists, rope-walkers, argonauts,
Avators, tamers of steel-birds and fugitives
From dream and reality, emigrants, mourners,
And each with his Shadow, to prove that Man lives;

And with them come gaps into listening Darkness:
The Gun-men, the molochs, the matadors, man-eaters,
Hiding in islands of loneliness, each one
Infections of hatred, and greed-plague, and fear.

For the season of red pyromaniacs, the dog-days
Are here, and now even the sun of a kiss
Sets a city on fire, and the innocent roses
Are the fever of foolish world-summers; and this

Beloved of my skeleton laughed, and said ' Tell me—
Why give me your heart like an eagle that flies,
Or a sun?—You should give me a crow for my dinner,
Or a flat dirty penny to lay on my eyes.'

And how can I save the heart of my Eden
That is only the hammering heart of the town,
When the only world left is my skeleton's city
Where the sun of the desert will never go down?

She has hearkened the Spider's prudence, the wisdom
That, spinning a foul architecture, unfurled
From his belly a city he made out of Hunger—
Constructed for Hunger's need: his is the world.

So what can I give to her? Civilisation's
Disease, a delirium flushed like the rose
And noisy as summer? Hands thumbless from unuse
—(From pads like a tiger's what bright claw grows?)

Though faithless the rose and the flesh, yet the city,
That eternal landscape, the skeleton's plan,
Has hope for its worm. . . . I will give her the pity
For the fallen Ape, of the Tiger, Man.

For my Eden is withered. I, damned by the Rainbow,
Near that fouled trodden alley, the bed where she lies,
Can wake no false dawn,—where, for want of a penny,
She lies with the sins of the world on her eyes."

Song

Once my heart was a summer rose
That cares not for right or wrong,
And the sun was another rose, that year,
They shone, the sun and the rose, my dear—
Over the long and the light summer land
All the bright summer long.

As I walked in the long and the light summer land,
All that I knew of shade
Was the cloud, my ombrelle of rustling grey
Sharp silk, it had spokes of grey steel rain—
Hiding my rose away, my dear,
Hiding my rose away.

And my laughter shone like a flight of birds
All in the summer gay,—
Tumbling pigeons and chattering starlings
And other pretty darlings, my dear,
And other pretty darlings.

To my heart like a rose, a rain of tears
(All the bright summer long)
Was only the sheen on a wood-dove's breast,
And sorrow only her song, my love—
And sorrow only my rest.

I passed a while in Feather Town—
(All the bright summer long)—
The idle wind puffed that town up
In air, then blew it down.

I walk alone now in Lead Town
(All in the summer gay . . .)
Where the steady people walk like the Dead—
And will not look my way.

For withering my heart, that summer rose,
Came another heart like a sun,—
And it drank all the dew from the rose, my love,
And the birds have forgotten their song
That sounded all summer long, my dear—
All the bright summer long.

Tattered Serenade: Beggar to Shadow

To Robert Herring

("*Je m'en allais, les poings dans mes poches crevées ;
Mon paletot aussi devenait idéal ;
J'allais sous le ciel, Muse, et j'étais ton féal.
Oh là là, que d'amours splendides j'ai rêvées.*"

ARTHUR RIMBAUD)

I

THESE are the nations of the Dead, their million-year-old
Rags about them,— these, the eternally cold,
Misery's worlds, with Hunger, their long sun
Shut in by polar worlds of ice, known to no other,
Without a name, without a brother,
Though their skin shows that they yet are men,

Airing their skeletons' well-planned cities where,
Left by the rose, the flesh, with truth alone,
The fevers of the world and of the heart,
The light of the sun, are gone.

And to their only friend, the Shade
They cast, their muttering voices sing this Serenade :

" O Shade ! Gigantic and adaptable Ape,
With the elegance of the skeleton
In your black tattered cape—
How like, and yet how unlike, you are to our last state !

You, too, have giant hands,— but have no thumbs
In a world where nothing is to make or hold,
Nor have you that appalling gulf the heart,—
Or that red gulf the gullet where only Hunger comes.

For face, you have a hollow wolf-grey cowl
Like mine . . . no voice to howl—

(O plain of winter wolves beneath my heart !)
And no identity ! No face to weep !
No bed—unlike the rich men who can creep
Into the pocks made by that vast disease
That is our civilisation, once there, lie at ease !

No memory,—no years,
Nothing to feel or think,
No friend from whom to part with youthful tears.
But your unutterable tatters cannot stink !

My overcoat, like yours, is an Ideal,
With a gulf for pockets—nothing there to steal
But my empty hands, that long have lost their use,
With nothing now to make, or hold, or lose.

Yet when spring comes, a world is in my head,
And dreams, for those who never have a bed—

The thought of a day when all may be possible,—all
May come my way," said small Rag-Castle to Rag-
                                      Castle tall. —
The young, that have no covering between
Their outer tatters and the worthless skin
That shows the air, the rain, they yet are men,

When remembering it is spring, falls the warm rain
Like lilies of the vale,
Buds golden-pale
Sprouting from pavements, or a universe of coins,
                                      endless gold

Pelting the homeless, those who have no dress
Against the winter cold,
But the skeleton, that burgh of idleness
Where only the worm works . . . those that are alone
Except for hunger, thirst, and lust;
For the fevers of the world and of the heart,
The summer rose, are gone.

Tattered Serenade: Beggar to Shadow

II

In the summer, when noone is cold,
And the country roads seem of hot gold,

While the air seems a draught of white wine
Where all day long golden stars shine,—

And the sun is a world of red meat
For those who have nothing to eat,

I walk the world, envying the roads
That have somewhere to go, that bear loads

Of happiness, business, and sorrow,
And the rose that cares not for tomorrow;

But I've nothing to hold or to lose,
And my hands have long since lost their use;

While my overcoat's but an Ideal,—
In my pockets there's nothing to steal.

But the roads have north, east, west, and south,
For their food, though I've none for my mouth

Or my empty red gulf of a heart—
I have no friend from whom I must part

But the shade that I cast,—my one friend
Till at last the world comes to an end.

His face is a wolfish grey cowl
Like my own, but without the wolf's howl,

For like me, he's a face, but no tears
He can shed, neither memory nor years.

But the Shadow has never known cold,
And the Shadow will never grow old,—

The black tatters he wears cannot stink
And he neither can feel, fear, or think,

While a universe grows in my head,—
I have dreams, though I have not a bed—

The thought of a world and a day
When all may be possible, still come my way

As I walk the long roads of hot gold
In the summer, when noone is cold.

Tears

To Pavel Tchelitchew

(". . . Methusalem, with all his hundreds of years, was but a mushroom of a night's growth, to this day; and all the fair monarchies, with all their thousands of years, and all the powerful Kings and the beautiful Queens of this world, were but as a bed of flowers, some gathered at six, some at seven, some at eight, all in one morning, in respect of this day."—JOHN DONNE, Sermon LXXIII.)

My tears were Orion's splendour with sextuple suns and
                               the million
Flowers in the fields of the heaven, where solar systems
                               are setting,—
The rocks of great diamonds in the midst of the clear wave
By May dews and early light ripened, more diamonds
                               begetting.
I wept for the glories of air, for the millions of dawns
And the splendours within Man's heart with the
                               darkness warring,
I wept for the beautiful queens of the world, like a
                               flower-bed shining,—
Now gathered, some at six, some at seven, but all in
                               Eternity's morning.
But now my tears have shrunk and like hours are falling:
I weep for Venus whose body has changed to a
                               metaphysical city
Whose heart-beat is now the sound of the revolutions,—
                               for love changed
To the hospital mercy, the scientists' hope for the future,
And for darkened Man, that complex multiplicity
Of air and water, plant and animal,
Hard diamond, infinite sun.

The Flowering Forest

THEY walked in the green wood, wild snows, soft,
                              unchilling,
Falling upon their hair, touching their lips
In the undying ways, in the bright April land.
" See, Aldebaran and wild Cassopeia
And Sirius are jealous of your white hand,—
Orion with sextuple suns and great nebulae
Procyon and Vega and Altair, the parallax
Trail of the fixed stars are falling to greet you.
While the planetary systems and snows on the branches
Are shaking with laughter at seeing the old
World's follies that dream that the heart will grow cold.
And the drops of dew fall'n from the branches and
                              white flowers,
Are young worlds that run to each other, their beings
Are one, in the green ways, the bright April land."

How Many Heavens . . .

("... *The Stancarest will needs have God not only to be in everything, but to be everything, that God is an angel in an angel, and a stone in a stone, and a straw in a straw.*"—JOHN DONNE, Sermon VII.)

THE emeralds are singing on the grasses
And in the trees the bells of the long cold are ringing,—
My blood seems changed to emeralds like the spears
Of grass beneath the earth piercing and singing.

The flame of the first blade
Is an angel piercing through the earth to sing
" God is everything !
The grass within the grass, the angel in the angel, flame
Within the flame, and He is the green shade that came
To be the heart of shade."

The grey-beard angel of the stone,
Who has grown wise with age, cried " Not alone
Am I within my silence,— God is the stone in the still
                                  stone, the silence laid
In the heart of silence " . . . then, above the glade

The yellow straws of light
Whereof the sun has built his nest, cry " Bright
Is the world, the yellow straw
My brother,— God is the straw within the straw :—
                                  All things are Light."

He is the sea of ripeness and the sweet apple's emerald lore.
So you, my flame of grass, my root of the world from which
                                  all Spring shall grow,
O you, my hawthorn bough of the stars, now leaning low
Through the day, for your flowers to kiss my lips, shall know
He is the core of the heart of love, and He, beyond labouring
                                  seas, our ultimate shore.

Spring

Deep in the shade, the starved man's cloak through
                     which the cold wind comes,
The shade, the only comfort of the slums,
The lost men, little children of this world
Where only the spider pities them, weaves from its thread
Their blankets against the cold, and where for bread
They have the stones of the ruins, cry to Death:
" There is no more to take, but my last breath.
O Death, thou art an outcast, too, like me —
Thou knowest I have nothing left but thee:
My only friend, shun not such raggedness
As the grave knows, and thy own loneliness.
Thou hast known hunger too: come then and hold
Me fast, till I no more shall feel the world's long cold:
Once thou didst steal my mother's milk from me,
But now, grown famished too, I pity thee."
Then with his universal smile, Death said,
" Outcast no more, for Man has made me God,
                        dreaming that God is dead."
Yet once, in spring, men's hearts forgot that they are cold,
And shone like many suns, — the dust seemed old,
No more a king, and powerless to hold
Endurance, hope, the loved and youthful smile.
The fields forgot that huntsmen snare
For Man, his brother the small hare,
The lame and lonely Dark forgot
That hungered, it must snare and plot, —
In that green spring, when hearts were warm for a
                     small fading while. . . .

You, the Young Rainbow

You, the young Rainbow of my tears, the gentle Halcyon
Over the troubled waters of my heart—
Lead now, as long ago, my grief, your flock, over the hollow
Hills to the far pastures of lost heaven.
But they are withered, the meadows and the horizon
Of the gentle Halcyon, hyacinthine sun.
Cold are the boughs, the constellations falling
From the spring branches; and your heart is far
And cold as Arcturus, the distance of all light-years
From the flowering earth and darkness of my heart.

Song

WE are the darkness in the heat of the day,
The rootless flowers in the air, the coolness : we are
                                                the water
Lying upon the leaves before Death, our sun,
And its vast heat has drunken us . . . Beauty's daughter
The heart of the rose and we are one.

We are the summer's children, the breath of evening,
                                                the days
When all may be hoped for,—we are the unreturning
Smile of the lost one, seen through the summer leaves—
That sun and its false light scorning.

The Youth with the Red-Gold Hair

*(" Did ghosts from those thickets walk about your land
So the tent of the shepherdess was cumbered with gold armour
Till the hero left your mother and turned back into the glade,
Bright as his armour ? "*

SACHEVERELL SITWELL)

THE gold-armoured ghost from the Roman road
Sighed over the wheat
" Fear not the sound and the glamour
Of my gold armour—
(The sound of the wind and the wheat)
Fear not its clamour. . . .
Fear only the red-gold sun with the fleece of a fox
Who will steal the fluttering bird you hide in your breast.
Fear only the red-gold rain
That will dim your brightness, O my tall tower of the corn,
You,—my blonde girl. . . ."
But the wind sighed " Rest." . . .
The wind in his grey knight's armour
The wind in his grey night armour
Sighed over the fields of the wheat, " He is gone. . . .
                                          . . . Forlorn."

The Night before Great Babylon . . .

THE night before great Babylon
Fell like the summer rain,
Under the great grey towers of the apple trees
Voices sounded again.
" O my root of life from which all branches grow -
Where the sun and moon for fruits hang low
Among worlds and waters for leaves,—lovely as Shade
                                              are you—
Or the lady who plucked an apple sparkling as the breeze
For her love. . . . So you give me your kiss
From which all worlds arise." . . . But a wind through
                                              the trees
Blew it away again.
" It is cold, and begins to rain ! "
" Not only the rain is falling."

" Greater are you than the rough Sun—
A warrior in his golden armour—
And the night is but your palace wall,"
Said she. . . . But a wind came tall,
The wind in his grey knight's armour,
The wind in his grey night armour—
And the great gold Sun was slain.
" What is the wind that doth blow ?
It is cold, and begins to rain."
" Not only the rain is falling."

Song

When I was but a child, that Lion
The Sun came, shaking his gold mane :
" From strength comes sweetness ; so, my Zion,
Your strong heart is my honeycomb,

And your soul is my Happy Land—
Although they call your heart a stone,
It is the stone from David's sling ;
And though you walk alone,

Seeing the starved man as a king,
Eating your heart within the shade
That man has cast, that folly made,
And digging water for the damned
From desert hearts, waste heavens and heights,
Your lion-like heart of burning gold
Shall seem my own.

And in your soul, my Happy Land,
Shall be my shaken mane of gold :
Man's dark shall tremble at my paw,—
Time's thunders change into the sand
Whereon I lie and roar."

Most Lovely Shade

Most lovely Dark, my Aethiopia born
Of the shade's richest splendour, leave not me
Where in the pomp and splendour of the shade
The dark air's leafy plumes no more a lulling music made.

Dark is your fleece, and dark the airs that grew
Amid those weeping leaves.
Plantations of the East drop precious dew
That, ripened by the light, rich leaves perspire.
Such are the drops that from the dark airs' feathers flew.

Most lovely Shade . . . Syrinx and Dryope
And that smooth nymph that changed into a tree
Are dead . . . the shade, that Aethiopia, sees
Their beauty make more bright its treasuries—
Their amber blood in porphyry veins still grows
Deep in the dark secret of the rose
And the smooth stem of many a weeping tree,
And in your beauty grows.

Come then, my pomp and splendour of the shade,
Most lovely cloud that the hot sun made black
As dark-leaved airs,—
          Come then, O precious cloud,
Lean to my heart : no shade of a rich tree
Shall pour such splendour as your heart to me.

The Weeping Rose

THE sorrowful rose in her deep night of leaves
Sighed " Weep no more :
See how I shine like the first light of tears,—
So let your sorrow be
Only the sound that grieves when honeyed rains
And amber blood flush all my sharp green veins :
So let your rose-shaped heart
Feel the first flush of summer, love's first smart
Is no more sorrowful than the deep tears
I weep within this green and honeyed clime.
But the green century of summer rains
Lay on the leaves, and like the rose I wept.
For love, my gardener, with green fingers stroked my
                                              leaves,
Like the gold wind of the south, deflowered my heart,
And now is gone :
In this empire of the shade I am alone.
O rose-shaped heart, now only the summer knows
If your poor amber dust was once a nymph, a heart, or but
                                              a summer rose."

The Swans

In the green light of water, like the day
Under green boughs, the spray
And air-pale petals of the foam seem flowers,—
Dark-leaved arbutus blooms with wax-pale bells
And their faint honey-smells,
The velvety syringa with smooth leaves,
Gloxinia with a green shade in the snow,
Jasmine and moon-clear orange-blossoms and green blooms
Of the wild strawberries from the shade of woods.
Their showers
Pelt the white women under the green trees,
Venusia, Cosmopolita, Pistillarine—
White solar statues, white rose-trees in snow
Flowering for ever, child-women, half stars
Half flowers, waves of the sea, born of a dream.

Their laughter flying through the trees like doves,
These angels come to watch their whiter ghosts
In the air-pale water, archipelagos
Of stars and young thin moons from great wings falling
As ripples widen.
These are their ghosts, their own white angels these!
O great wings spreading—
Your bones are made of amber, smooth and thin
Grown from the amber dust that was a rose
Or nymph in swan-smooth waters.
                              But Time's winter falls
With snows as soft, as soundless . . . Then, who knows
Rose-footed swan from snow, or girl from rose?

Note.—Lines 12, 13, 14, 15, and 16 are a rough adaptation into English of a prose passage by Paul Eluard.

31

An Old Woman

I, AN old woman in the light of the sun,
Wait for my Wanderer, and my upturned face
Has all the glory of the remembering Day
The hallowed grandeur of the primeval clay
That knew the Flood, and suffered all the dryness
Of the uncaring heaven, the sun its lover.

For the sun is the first lover of the world,
Blessing all humble creatures, all life-giving,
Blessing the end of life and the work done,
The clean and the unclean, ores in earth, and splendours
Within the heart of man, that second sun.

For when the first founts and deep waterways
Of the young light flow down and lie like peace
Upon the upturned faces of the blind
From life, it comes to bless
Eternity in its poor mortal dress,—
Shining upon young lovers and old lechers
Rising from their beds, and laying gold
Alike in the unhopeful path of beggars
And in the darkness of the miser's heart.
The crookèd has a shadow light made straight,
The shallow places gain their strength again,—
And desert hearts, waste heavens, the barren height
Forget that they are cold.
The man-made chasms between man and man
Of creeds and tongues are fill'd, the guiltless light
Remakes all men and things in holiness.

And he who blessed the fox with a golden fleece
And covered earth with ears of corn like the planets

32

Bearded with thick ripe gold,
For the holy bread of mankind, blessed my clay :
For the sun cares not that I am a simple woman,
To him, laughing, the veins in my arms and the wrinkles
From work on my nursing hands are sacred as branches
And furrows of harvest . . . to him, the heat of the earth
And beat of the heart are one,—
Born from the energy of the world, the love
That keeps the Golden Ones in their place above,
And hearts and blood of beasts even in motion,—
Without which comets, sun, plants, and all living beings
And warmth in the inward parts of the earth would freeze.
And the sun does not care if I live in holiness,
To him, my mortal dress
Is sacred, part of the earth, a lump of the world
With my splendours, ores, impurities, and harvest,
Over which shines my heart, that ripening sun.

Though the dust, the shining racer, overtake me,
I too was a golden woman like those that walk
In the fields of the heavens :—but am now grown old
And must sit by the fire and watch the fire grow cold,
—A country Fate whose spool is the household task.
Yet still I am loved by the sun, and still am part
Of earth. In the evenings bringing home the workers,
Bringing the wanderer home and the dead child,
The child unborn and never to be conceived,
Home to the mother's breast, I sit by the fire
Where the seed of gold drops dead and the kettle simmers
With a sweet sound like that of a hive of bees,
And I wait for my Wanderer to come home to rest—
Covered with earth as if he had been working
Among the happy gardens, the holy fields
Where the bread of mankind ripens in the stillness.

Unchanged to me by death, I shall hold to my breast
My little child in his sleep, I shall seem the consoling
Earth, the mother of corn, nurse of the unreturning.

Wise is the earth, consoling grief and glory,
The golden heroes proud as pomp of waves,—
Great is the earth embracing them, their graves,
And great is the earth's story.
For though the soundless wrinkles fall like snow
On many a golden cheek, and creeds grow old
And change,—man's heart, that sun,
Outlives all terrors shaking the old night:
The world's huge fevers burn and shine, turn cold,
Yet the heavenly bodies and young lovers burn and shine,
The golden lovers walk in the holy fields
Where the Abraham-bearded sun, the father of all things
Is shouting of ripeness, and the whole world of dews and
                                splendours are singing
To the cradles of earth, of men, beasts, harvests, swinging
In the peace of God's heart.   And I, the primeval clay
That has known earth's grief and harvest's happiness,
Seeing mankind's dark seed-time, come to bless,—
Forgive and bless all men like the holy light.

THE END.

Printed in Great Britain by R. & R. CLARK, LIMITED, *Edinburgh.*